TOP 100
THINGS
~~TEENAGERS~~
SHOULD KNOW
everyone

A Beautiful, Bold Guide to
Growing Up with Wisdom,
Courage, and Heart

Dr. Christopher Graham, PhD., CCHT

LIBRARY & ARCHIVES CANADA
ISBN 978-1-998517-80-0

Mind: Thinking, Learning, and Mental Growth

1. You are not your thoughts—you are the one observing them.
2. Curiosity is a superpower.
3. Your brain grows stronger every time you challenge it.
4. It's okay not to know—asking questions is brave.
5. Critical thinking protects you from manipulation.
6. Intelligence comes in many forms—emotional, creative, logical, etc.
7. Learn how you learn best—visual, auditory, kinesthetic, etc.
8. Boredom often leads to creativity.
9. Focus is a skill you can train.
10. You can change your mind—it's a sign of growth, not weakness.

Emotions: Emotional Intelligence & Resilience

11. Emotions are messengers, not enemies.

12. You don't have to act on every feeling.

13. It's okay to cry—it's a reset, not a breakdown.

14. You can feel two things at once—joy and sadness can coexist.

15. Not everyone will like you, and that's okay.

16. Boundaries are an act of self-respect.

17. Apologizing when you're wrong is strength, not shame.

18. You are allowed to walk away from toxic energy.

19. Your feelings are valid—even when others don't understand them.

20. You are not alone in your struggles—even when it feels like it.

Spirit: Identity, Purpose & Inner Compass

21. You are more than your labels.

22. You have a voice worth hearing.

23. You were born with purpose—uncovering it is the journey.

24. Comparison steals joy.

25. You are not behind—you're on your own timeline.

26. Your intuition is wise—listen to it.

27. Stillness reveals what noise hides.

28. You are enough—even when you're doing nothing.

29. The world needs your authenticity, not your perfection.

30. You are a soul having a human experience.

Relationships: Family, Friends & Social Wisdom

31. Choose friends who feel like sunlight.

32. It's okay to outgrow people.

33. Communication is more about listening than speaking.

34. You don't owe anyone access to your peace.

35. Not everyone deserves to know your story.

36. Loyalty to yourself comes before loyalty to others.

37. Love is action, not just words.

38. Forgiveness frees *you*.

39. You can learn from every relationship—even the painful ones.

40. Empathy changes everything.

Life Skills: Practical & Financial Intelligence

41. Learn how to cook at least 3 meals from scratch.

42. Know how to manage a basic budget.

43. Save at least 10% of everything you earn.

44. Learn how to read contracts before signing anything.

45. Credit cards are not free money—understand interest.

46. Know how to do laundry, sew a button, and clean a space.

47. Time is more valuable than money.

48. Plan long-term but act short-term.

49. The internet remembers everything—post wisely.

50. Learn how to write a strong email and a résumé.

Technology & Media Literacy

51. Not everything you see online is real.

52. Social media is a highlight reel, not reality.

53. Digital detox is powerful—your brain needs breaks.

54. You are the product in most free apps.

55. Learn how to identify reliable sources.

56. What you post today may affect your future.

57. Algorithms show you more of what you *engage* with—choose consciously.

58. Not every message deserves a response.

59. Protect your passwords like you would a key.

60. Create more than you consume.

Body & Wellness

61. Your body is your home—treat it with love.

62. Sleep is not optional for growth—prioritize it.

63. Movement isn't just exercise—it's medicine.

64. Eat to nourish, not to punish.

65. Water solves more problems than we think.

66. Your body is changing, and that's natural.

67. What you consume (food, media, energy) affects how you feel.

68. Rest is productive.

69. Hormones can distort perception—pause before reacting.

70. There's strength in caring for yourself.

Creativity & Expression

71. Art heals—even if no one sees it.

72. Dance, sing, write—express without apology.

73. Creativity is a muscle—use it often.

74. Your story matters—even if you think it's "normal."

75. Journaling clears the mind and awakens the soul.

76. What you make doesn't have to be perfect to be powerful.

77. Learn to appreciate art—it unlocks empathy.

78. You can invent your own rituals and meaning.

79. Self-expression is a rebellion against numbness.

80. The world needs your weird.

Challenges, Mistakes & Growth

81. Failure is feedback, not defeat.
82. Everyone makes mistakes—own yours and learn from them.
83. Resilience is built, not born.
84. You grow through what you go through.
85. Hard times don't last—but they shape you.
86. Struggles don't mean you're broken—they mean you're becoming.
87. You're allowed to start over.
88. Pain can be a teacher.
89. Not everything is meant to be fixed—some things are meant to be felt.
90. Every scar tells a story of survival.

Wonder, Mystery & Spirituality

91. Life is stranger and more magical than it seems.

92. There's wisdom in silence.

93. Look at the stars—they're part of your story.

94. Nature reflects what you need to hear.

95. Miracles happen quietly.

96. You don't need all the answers to have faith.

97. Dreams carry messages—listen.

98. Ask the big questions—even if there are no easy answers.

99. You are connected to something greater.

100. Your light matters in this world.

MIND
Thinking, Learning, and Mental Growth

"You are the sky. Everything else – it's just the weather."
– Pema Chödrön

This quote reminds you that no matter how chaotic your thoughts or emotions become, your true self remains steady beneath them. The sky doesn't try to control the weather—it allows everything to pass through. In the same way, you don't need to fight every feeling. You are the awareness behind it all.

What "weather" have you been experiencing lately—and how can you reconnect with the sky within you?

_____

_____

_____

_____

_____

_____

_____

_____

_____

1. You are not your thoughts—you are the one observing them.

You don't have to believe every thought that passes through your mind. Thoughts can be anxious, angry, self-critical, or even joyful—but none of them define you. The real you is the awareness behind them. Once you learn to observe your thoughts instead of becoming them, you gain power over your reactions and clarity about who you really are.

What thought have you been identifying with lately—and what happens when you just observe it instead?

_____

_____

_____

_____

_____

_____

_____

_____

_____

_____

2. Curiosity is a superpower.

Being curious means you're open to learning, exploring, and growing. It's the fuel behind creativity, science, empathy, and adventure. When you follow curiosity instead of fear, the world opens up in ways you never expected.

What's something you're curious about right now— and how can you explore it further?

_____

_____

_____

_____

_____

_____

_____

_____

_____

_____

_____

_____

_____

3. Your brain grows stronger every time you challenge it.

Each time you work through a problem, struggle to understand something, or push beyond your comfort zone, you literally rewire your brain. This is called neuroplasticity. Challenges aren't signs of failure—they're signs your brain is evolving.

What's one challenge you've faced that helped you grow mentally?

_____
_____
_____
_____
_____
_____
_____
_____
_____
_____
_____
_____
_____
_____

4. It's okay not to know—asking questions is brave.

There's strength in not knowing something—because that's the first step to learning. Asking a question isn't a sign of weakness; it's a signal that you care enough to grow. The people who change the world are the ones who ask, 'Why?'

What's one question you've been holding back from asking—and what might happen if you did?

_____
_____
_____
_____
_____
_____
_____
_____
_____
_____
_____
_____
_____

5. Critical thinking protects you from manipulation.

We live in a world full of opinions, ads, and algorithms trying to sway your thinking. Critical thinking helps you pause, analyze, and decide for yourself what's true. It's like having a mental shield that protects your choices and your values.

When was the last time you paused to question what you were being told?

_____

_____

_____

_____

_____

_____

_____

_____

_____

_____

_____

_____

_____

_____

6. Intelligence comes in many forms—emotional, creative, logical, etc.

Some people shine in numbers, others in music, emotion, movement, or nature. There's no one way to be smart. When you understand your unique type of intelligence, you stop trying to fit in and start building where you stand out.

What kind of intelligence do you most resonate with—and how are you using it?

_____

_____

_____

_____

_____

_____

_____

_____

_____

_____

_____

_____

_____

7. Learn how you learn best—visual, auditory, kinesthetic.

Some people remember best when they hear, others when they see or do. Knowing your learning style helps you study smarter, not harder. It's like having a map to your brain—and once you know the terrain, everything gets easier.

What's one way you can adjust your learning to match your style more effectively?

_____

_____

_____

_____

_____

_____

_____

_____

_____

_____

_____

_____

8. Boredom often leads to creativity.

That feeling of 'I'm so bored' often comes right before a breakthrough. When your brain has space and no distractions, it starts to play, imagine, and invent. Boredom isn't a void—it's the spark before a creative fire.

Next time you're bored, what creative outlet could you try instead of distracting yourself?

_____

_____

_____

_____

_____

_____

_____

_____

_____

_____

_____

_____

9. Focus is a skill you can train.

Focus is like a flashlight—you can point it where you choose. In a noisy world full of distractions, training your attention is one of the most valuable skills you can have. Focus builds discipline, peace, and power.

How could you practice sharpening your focus in your daily life?

_____

_____

_____

_____

_____

_____

_____

_____

_____

_____

_____

_____

_____

_____

_____

10. You can change your mind—it's a sign of growth, not weakness.

Changing your mind doesn't mean you're weak or fake—it means you're learning. As you grow, you'll gain new insights, face new truths, and develop new values. Let yourself evolve without guilt—that's wisdom in motion.

What's something you've changed your mind about—and how did it help you grow?

_____

_____

_____

_____

_____

_____

_____

_____

_____

_____

_____

_____

_____

EMOTIONS
Emotional Intelligence & Resilience

"Feelings are much like waves, we can't stop them from coming but we can choose which ones to surf."

— Jonatan Mårtensson

Emotions come and go, sometimes intensely, sometimes gently. The key is learning which feelings to ride with and which ones to let pass. You don't have to engage with every wave. This is how you protect your energy and grow emotional strength.

Which emotions have you been riding lately—and which ones could you let pass by?

_____

_____

_____

_____

_____

_____

_____

_____

_____

11. Emotions are messengers, not enemies.

Your feelings serve as important signals about your inner state. Instead of fighting or ignoring them, try to listen carefully to what they're telling you. They can guide you in understanding your needs and in addressing issues before they grow.

What emotion has been trying to tell you something lately?

_____

_____

_____

_____

_____

_____

_____

_____

_____

_____

_____

_____

12. You don't have to act on every feeling.

Not every emotion demands an immediate reaction.
When you pause and consider your options, you
empower yourself to choose responses that truly align
with your values. This mindful approach builds inner
strength and clarity.

*What's one recent emotion you could acknowledge
without reacting to it?*

_____

_____

_____

_____

_____

_____

_____

_____

_____

_____

_____

_____

_____

13. It's okay to cry—it's a reset, not a breakdown.

Crying is a natural and healthy way to process intense feelings. Far from being a sign of weakness, it's a powerful release that cleanses and resets your emotional state. Embrace your tears as part of healing.

When was the last time you let yourself release through tears?

_____

_____

_____

_____

_____

_____

_____

_____

_____

_____

_____

_____

_____

14. You can feel two things at once—joy and sadness can coexist.

Our emotional landscape is rich and multifaceted. Sometimes, you might experience conflicting feelings at the same time. Embrace this complexity—it's a reminder that life isn't just black or white but filled with beautiful shades of gray.

What's a moment where you felt mixed emotions— and what did it teach you?

_____

_____

_____

_____

_____

_____

_____

_____

_____

_____

_____

_____

_____

15. Not everyone will like you, and that's okay.

It's impossible to please everyone, and seeking universal approval can be exhausting. Instead, focus on being true to yourself. Your authenticity is your strength, and those who resonate with you will value you for exactly who you are.

How much of your energy is spent trying to be liked—and what would shift if you let that go?

_____

_____

_____

_____

_____

_____

_____

_____

_____

_____

_____

_____

_____

_____

16. Boundaries are an act of self-respect.

Setting boundaries is not selfish—it's essential for your well-being. Clearly defining what you're comfortable with protects your energy and ensures that others treat you with the respect you deserve.

Where in your life could you benefit from setting a clearer boundary?

_____

_____

_____

_____

_____

_____

_____

_____

_____

_____

_____

_____

_____

_____

_____

17. Apologizing when you're wrong is strength, not shame.

Acknowledging mistakes and offering a sincere apology takes courage. It shows that you value growth and authenticity over pride. Admitting faults helps build trust and fosters personal development.

Is there someone you owe a sincere apology to—and what's holding you back?

_____

_____

_____

_____

_____

_____

_____

_____

_____

_____

_____

_____

_____

_____

18. You are allowed to walk away from toxic energy.

Sometimes, preserving your peace means stepping away from situations or people that drain you. Walking away isn't giving up—it's choosing to protect your mental and emotional health for your own growth.

What's draining you that you might need to step away from?

_____

_____

_____

_____

_____

_____

_____

_____

_____

_____

_____

_____

_____

19. Your feelings are valid—even when others don't understand them.

Your emotions are uniquely yours, and they matter. Even
if others can't fully relate, honoring your feelings is key to self-compassion and healing. Trust that what you feel is real and significant.

What's draining you that you might need to step away from?

_____

_____

_____

_____

_____

_____

_____

_____

_____

_____

_____

_____

20. You are not alone in your struggles—even when it feels like it.

Everyone faces challenges, even if it sometimes feels like you're on your own. Recognizing that struggle is a shared human experience can bring comfort and encourage you to reach out for support when needed.

Who could you reach out to or open up to today, even just a little?

_____

_____

_____

_____

_____

_____

_____

_____

_____

_____

_____

_____

_____

SPIRIT

Identity, Purpose & Inner Compass

"Don't ask what the world needs. Ask what makes you come alive and go do it."

— Howard Thurman

Purpose doesn't come from pressure—it comes from passion. You were made to feel alive. That aliveness is the real gift you offer. It shifts your focus from obligation to inspiration and reminds you that your joy is part of your purpose.

What makes you feel most alive—and how can you bring more of that into your everyday life?

_____

_____

_____

_____

_____

_____

_____

_____

_____

21. You are more than your labels.

Labels can describe aspects of who you are, but they don't capture your entire being. You are a growing, evolving human with depth and layers that can't be summed up in a word. Don't shrink yourself to fit into someone else's box.

What label have you outgrown—and what could take its place?

_____
_____
_____
_____
_____
_____
_____
_____
_____
_____
_____
_____
_____
_____

22. You have a voice worth hearing.

Your thoughts, feelings, and experiences matter. Whether you speak loudly or quietly, your voice has the power to shift minds, comfort hearts, and inspire change. Don't underestimate what you have to say.

What's something you've been wanting to say—but haven't yet?

_____
_____
_____
_____
_____
_____
_____
_____
_____
_____
_____
_____
_____
_____

23. You were born with purpose—uncovering it is the journey.

You don't have to have everything figured out. Life is a process of discovery, and your purpose might shift and grow with you. Keep following what lights you up. That's where the clues are.

What lights you up—and how can you follow that feeling today?

_____

_____

_____

_____

_____

_____

_____

_____

_____

_____

_____

_____

24. Comparison steals joy.

When you constantly measure yourself against others, you rob yourself of peace. Everyone's path is different. Stay in your lane and nurture your growth—you'll thrive in ways comparison could never offer.

Who or what have you been comparing yourself to—and how could you shift focus back to yourself?

_____

_____

_____

_____

_____

_____

_____

_____

_____

_____

_____

_____

_____

25. You are not behind—you're on your own timeline.

Life isn't a race, and there is no set schedule for success or self-discovery. You're exactly where you need to be right now. Trust your timing—it's wiser than you think.

What expectation could you release to feel more aligned with your pace?

_____

_____

_____

_____

_____

_____

_____

_____

_____

_____

_____

_____

_____

_____

_____

_____

26. Your intuition is wise—listen to it.

There's a quiet knowing inside you that speaks when you're still. It won't shout, but it will guide. The more you trust it, the more confident you'll become in your own path.

What is your gut quietly telling you—and are you listening?

_____

_____

_____

_____

_____

_____

_____

_____

_____

_____

_____

_____

_____

_____

_____

27. Stillness reveals what noise hides.

In the silence, you begin to hear your real thoughts and feel your real needs. Creating moments of stillness can help you reconnect to yourself in a world that never stops moving.

When was the last time you sat in stillness—and what surfaced?

_____
_____
_____
_____
_____
_____
_____
_____
_____
_____
_____
_____
_____
_____
_____

28. You are enough—even when you're doing nothing.

Your worth isn't tied to productivity, success, or approval. You are valuable simply because you exist. Rest, breathe, and let go of the pressure to prove yourself.

What would change if you truly believed your worth wasn't tied to productivity?

_____

_____

_____

_____

_____

_____

_____

_____

_____

_____

_____

_____

_____

_____

29. The world needs your authenticity, not your perfection.

Perfection is impossible, but you can be perfectly you and being authentic is powerful. When you show up as your true self—flaws and all—you give others permission to do the same. That's how real connection happens.

Where are you hiding your real self—and what might happen if you showed up fully?

_____

_____

_____

_____

_____

_____

_____

_____

_____

_____

_____

_____

30. You are a soul having a human experience.

You are more than your body, your circumstances, or your roles. You are a soul with depth, purpose, and inner light. Remembering this can help you stay grounded during hard times and inspired during joyful ones.

What helps you reconnect with the deeper part of who you are?

_____

_____

_____

_____

_____

_____

_____

_____

_____

_____

_____

_____

_____

RELATIONSHIPS
Family, Friends & Social Wisdom

"The only way to have a friend is to be one."
— Ralph Waldo Emerson

Friendship isn't something you find—it's something you give. Being kind, trustworthy, present, and supportive is how real connection grows. When you show up for others in meaningful ways, you naturally attract relationships rooted in mutual care and respect.

What qualities do you value in a friend—and how do you embody those qualities in your own life?

_____

_____

_____

_____

_____

_____

_____

_____

_____

_____

31. Healing is not linear.

There will be days when you feel like you've made progress and others when the pain resurfaces. That doesn't mean you're failing—it means you're human. Give yourself grace as you move forward in waves, not in straight lines.

What part of your healing journey can you offer more patience to?

_____

_____

_____

_____

_____

_____

_____

_____

_____

_____

_____

_____

32. Forgiveness frees you more than anyone else.

Holding onto resentment keeps you tied to pain. Forgiveness isn't about excusing bad behavior—it's about reclaiming your peace and letting go of what's weighing you down.

What resentment are you ready to let go of—for your own peace?

_____

_____

_____

_____

_____

_____

_____

_____

_____

_____

_____

_____

_____

_____

33. Vulnerability builds connection.

When you share your truth—your fears, dreams, and struggles—you invite others to do the same. Vulnerability breaks down walls and replaces them with bridges.

What's one truth you've been afraid to share—and who might understand it?

_____

_____

_____

_____

_____

_____

_____

_____

_____

_____

_____

_____

_____

_____

34. Dreams take time. Be patient with the process.

Every big dream is built through small, steady steps. It's okay if things don't happen overnight. What matters is that you keep showing up, even when progress feels slow.

What step can you take today—however small—that brings you closer to your dream?

_____

_____

_____

_____

_____

_____

_____

_____

_____

_____

_____

_____

_____

35. You're allowed to redefine yourself.

You're not locked into past decisions, identities, or mistakes. Every day is a chance to grow, shift, and become someone closer to your truth.

What's one part of your identity you'd like to evolve or release?

_____

_____

_____

_____

_____

_____

_____

_____

_____

_____

_____

_____

_____

_____

_____

_____

36. Creativity isn't about talent—it's about expression.

Creativity lives in all of us. It's not about being the best; it's about being honest. Whether through writing, music, movement, or doodling in a notebook, your voice deserves to be seen and heard.

What's one creative outlet you can try without judging the result?

_____

_____

_____

_____

_____

_____

_____

_____

_____

_____

_____

_____

_____

_____

37. Social media is a highlight reel, not real life.

You're often seeing someone's best moment—not their full story. Don't compare your behind-the-scenes to someone else's filtered version of reality.

How has social media shaped your self-perception—and how can you reclaim your perspective?

_____

_____

_____

_____

_____

_____

_____

_____

_____

_____

_____

_____

_____

_____

38. Alone doesn't mean lonely.

Being alone can be a sacred space to reflect, recharge, and reconnect with yourself. When you learn to enjoy your own company, you discover inner peace.

When was the last time you enjoyed your own company—and what did you discover?

_____

_____

_____

_____

_____

_____

_____

_____

_____

_____

_____

_____

_____

_____

_____

39. Confidence is built by keeping promises to yourself.

Each time you show up for yourself—whether by following through, setting boundaries, or choosing kindness—you grow stronger. Self-trust is the foundation of real confidence.

What promise can you make—and keep—to yourself today?

_____
_____
_____
_____
_____
_____
_____
_____
_____
_____
_____
_____
_____

40. Rest is not a reward—it's a requirement.

You don't have to earn your rest. Rest is essential for your body, mind, and spirit to heal, think, and thrive. Make it part of your rhythm, not just a reaction to burnout.

What would it look like to rest because you're worthy—not because you're worn out?

_____
_____
_____
_____
_____
_____
_____
_____
_____
_____
_____
_____
_____
_____
_____

LIFE SKILLS
Practical & Financial Intelligence

"Move forward. Aim High. Plan a takeoff. Don't just sit on the runway and hope someone will come along and push the airplane. Change your attitude and gain some altitude"

— Donald J. Trump

This quote is a bold reminder that waiting won't get you where you want to go. You are the pilot of your life. Planning, acting, and believing in yourself are what help you take flight. Your mindset is the engine. Your vision is the sky. Don't wait—take off

What's an area in your life where you've been waiting for a push—and what's one action you can take to lift off?

_____

_____

_____

_____

_____

_____

_____

_____

41. You teach people how to treat you.

Every time you set a boundary, speak up, or walk away from disrespect, you're showing others what's acceptable in your world. You don't have to tolerate unkindness just to keep the peace.

Where have you been tolerating less than you deserve—and what boundary needs to be set?

_____

_____

_____

_____

_____

_____

_____

_____

_____

_____

_____

_____

_____

_____

42. Gratitude changes perspective.

When you focus on what's working instead of what's missing, your entire outlook shifts. Gratitude doesn't erase hardship, but it brings light into even the darkest corners.

What are three things you're truly grateful for right now?

_____

_____

_____

_____

_____

_____

_____

_____

_____

_____

_____

_____

_____

_____

43. Struggle is part of the story—not the whole story.

Your hardest moments don't define you. They are chapters, not your entire book. Keep turning the page. The story isn't over.

What's one difficult chapter that helped shape who you are today?

_____

_____

_____

_____

_____

_____

_____

_____

_____

_____

_____

_____

_____

_____

_____

44. Saying no is a full sentence.

You don't owe anyone an explanation for taking care of your needs. Saying 'no' with kindness is one of the most powerful things you can do for your well-being.

Where do you need to say "no" in order to say "yes" to yourself?

_____

_____

_____

_____

_____

_____

_____

_____

_____

_____

_____

_____

_____

_____

45. You are not too much—you are just enough.

If someone tells you you're too loud, too sensitive, too ambitious—that might just mean you're more than they know how to handle. You don't need to shrink to make others comfortable.

What part of yourself have you been dimming—and how can you reclaim it?

_____

_____

_____

_____

_____

_____

_____

_____

_____

_____

_____

_____

_____

46. You can hold space for others without carrying their pain.

Empathy is beautiful, but it doesn't mean absorbing everyone else's suffering. You can love, support, and care while still protecting your own peace.

Where can you care with compassion but without self-sacrifice?

_____

_____

_____

_____

_____

_____

_____

_____

_____

_____

_____

_____

_____

_____

47. Growth often feels like discomfort.

When you're stretching into a new version of yourself, it can feel awkward or painful. That's not a sign to stop—it's a sign that you're transforming.

What discomfort are you sitting with now—and what might it be teaching you?

_____

_____

_____

_____

_____

_____

_____

_____

_____

_____

_____

_____

_____

_____

48. You are never too young to make a difference.

Age doesn't define your impact. Your ideas, your voice, and your passion matter now—not someday. Don't wait for permission to change the world.

What's one small action you can take today to create a ripple?

_____
_____
_____
_____
_____
_____
_____
_____
_____
_____
_____
_____
_____
_____

49. Change is scary—and also full of opportunity.

Every time you step into the unknown, you create space
for something new to grow. Fear is natural, but so is
courage. Let both walk beside you.

What change are you resisting—and what possibility
might be waiting on the other side?

_____

_____

_____

_____

_____

_____

_____

_____

_____

_____

_____

_____

_____

_____

_____

_____

50. You are your own best advocate.

Speak up for yourself. Ask questions. Say what you need. Nobody knows your inner world like you do, and your well-being is worth protecting.

What do you need right now—and how can you ask for it with clarity and courage?

_____

_____

_____

_____

_____

_____

_____

_____

_____

_____

_____

_____

_____

_____

_____

_____

_____

BODY & WELLNESS

"Take care of your body. It's the only place you have to live."

— Jim Rohn

Your body is more than just a vessel—it's your lifelong home. Every thought, feeling, and experience flows through it. How you treat your body effects every part of your life. When you nourish it, rest it, move it, and honor its signals, you create a strong, safe foundation for everything else you do.

What's one small way you can take better care of your body this week—and how might it affect your mind and spirit?

_____

_____

_____

_____

_____

_____

_____

_____

51. You can start over at any moment.

A fresh start doesn't require a new year, a perfect plan, or someone else's approval. Every breath, every morning, every decision is a chance to begin again. Let go of guilt and choose growth.

What's one area of your life that needs a reset—and what's your first step?

_____
_____
_____
_____
_____
_____
_____
_____
_____
_____
_____
_____
_____
_____

52. Your story is still being written.

Whatever you've faced, it's not the end of your story. You are still becoming, still unfolding. Don't let a single chapter convince you it's the whole book.

If this is just one chapter, what kind of story do you want to write next?

_____
_____
_____
_____
_____
_____
_____
_____
_____
_____
_____
_____
_____
_____
_____

53. Your energy is sacred—spend it wisely.

You only have so much time and energy in a day. Who and what you give it to shapes your life. Protect your spark. Spend your energy like it's the most valuable currency you have.

What or who is draining your energy—and how can you shift your investment?

_____
_____
_____
_____
_____
_____
_____
_____
_____
_____
_____
_____
_____
_____

54. Trust is earned, not owed.

You don't have to give your trust to everyone—and you're not wrong for being cautious. Trust builds through action, not words. Pay attention to consistency, not promises.

Who in your life has truly earned your trust—and how do they show it?

_____

_____

_____

_____

_____

_____

_____

_____

_____

_____

_____

_____

_____

_____

_____

55. Progress matters more than perfection.

Perfection is a moving target you'll never quite hit—but progress is real and powerful. Every step you take matters. Celebrate effort, not flawlessness.

What's one imperfect step forward you're proud of?

_____
_____
_____
_____
_____
_____
_____
_____
_____
_____
_____
_____
_____
_____
_____
_____

56. You don't have to prove your worth.

You are enough just as you are—not because of your grades, followers, or achievements, but because of your humanity. Breathe into that truth. You are worthy of love and belonging.

When do you feel most worthy—just as you are?

_____

_____

_____

_____

_____

_____

_____

_____

_____

_____

_____

_____

_____

_____

_____

57. Not everyone is meant to stay—and that's okay.

Some people are here for a season, to teach you something, to walk part of your path. Letting go doesn't mean failure—it means making space for new alignment.

Who or what are you being invited to release with love?

_____
_____
_____
_____
_____
_____
_____
_____
_____
_____
_____
_____
_____

58. You can't control everything—focus on what you can.

Trying to control the uncontrollable leads to frustration and burnout. Peace comes from directing your attention inward: your attitude, your response, your actions.

What's one thing within your control that you can take action on today?

_____

_____

_____

_____

_____

_____

_____

_____

_____

_____

_____

_____

_____

_____

59. You deserve boundaries, rest, and joy—just because.

You don't need to earn your right to feel good. You deserve to rest without guilt, to say no without apology, and to feel joy even when the world is heavy.

Where are you denying yourself joy or rest—and why?

_____

_____

_____

_____

_____

_____

_____

_____

_____

_____

_____

_____

_____

_____

_____

60. The best relationship you'll ever have is with yourself.

You are the one person you'll spend your entire life with. Learn to love your own company, speak kindly to yourself, and show up like someone worth investing in—because you are.

What's one way you can deepen your relationship with yourself today?

_____

_____

_____

_____

_____

_____

_____

_____

_____

_____

_____

_____

_____

_____

TECHNOLOGY
Media Literacy

"Technology is a useful servant but a dangerous master.'

        – Christian Lous Lange

Technology can help you learn, create, and connect—but only when you stay in control. When you let screens, apps, or algorithms dictate your time, choices, or identity, it stops being a tool and starts becoming a trap. The key is mindful use—tech should serve your life, not replace it.

Where in your life is technology helping you—and where might it be taking over more than it should?

_____

_____

_____

_____

_____

_____

_____

_____

_____

61. Technology is a tool, not a replacement for connection.

Phones and apps can help us stay in touch—but they can't replace the depth of a real conversation, a shared laugh, or silent support. Use tech to connect, not disconnect.

How can you use tech today to deepen a real connection, not replace one?

_____

_____

_____

_____

_____

_____

_____

_____

_____

_____

_____

_____

_____

62. Likes don't equal love.

Social media can't measure your worth. True connection isn't found in numbers—it's felt in presence, honesty, and real-life support. Don't trade your self-esteem for a heart icon.

Whose approval really matters—and are you seeking it in the right places?

_____

_____

_____

_____

_____

_____

_____

_____

_____

_____

_____

_____

_____

_____

63. Privacy is power.

Not everyone needs to know everything. Holding sacred space for your thoughts, feelings, and goals keeps your energy safe and centered. You're allowed to be selective.

What part of your life would benefit from more sacred privacy?

---

64. It's okay to unplug.

You're not missing out—you're tuning in. Time away from screens gives your mind a chance to rest and your spirit a chance to breathe. Your peace is more important than your notifications.

When could you give yourself space to unplug and just be?

_____
_____
_____
_____
_____
_____
_____
_____
_____
_____
_____
_____
_____
_____

65. You don't have to share everything online.

Some moments are too precious for a post. Not everything needs to be public. It's okay to live life for you, not for the algorithm.

What moment could you choose to keep just for yourself—and why might that feel freeing?

_____

_____

_____

_____

_____

_____

_____

_____

_____

_____

_____

_____

_____

_____

_____

66. Your digital footprint matters.

What you post reflects who you are becoming. Future employers, partners, and even your future self may look back one day. Post with intention—and self-respect.

What does your online presence say about your values and growth?

_____

_____

_____

_____

_____

_____

_____

_____

_____

_____

_____

_____

_____

_____

_____

_____

67. You control your feed—curate it for your well-being.

Follow people who inspire you. Mute or unfollow those who drain or distract you. What you see everyday shapes how you feel. Make it nourishing.

What could you remove or add to your digital space to better support your mental health?

_____

_____

_____

_____

_____

_____

_____

_____

_____

_____

_____

_____

_____

_____

68. The algorithm isn't your compass.

Just because it's trending doesn't mean it's truth. Your values matter more than virality. Don't let algorithms decide your identity.

Where are you letting trends steer you—and what would it look like to lead from your own truth?

_____

_____

_____

_____

_____

_____

_____

_____

_____

_____

_____

_____

_____

_____

_____

69. You're allowed to log off and reclaim your time.

You don't owe constant access to anyone. Rest, create, reflect—your real life matters more than your screen life.

How would your life feel if you spent less time online and more time tuned in to yourself?

_____

_____

_____

_____

_____

_____

_____

_____

_____

_____

_____

_____

_____

_____

_____

70. Use tech to create, not just consume.

Technology can be a tool for art, storytelling, activism, and connection. Don't just scroll—build. Use the digital world to express your light.

What could you build, share, or express today using your digital tools?

_____
_____
_____
_____
_____
_____
_____
_____
_____
_____
_____
_____
_____
_____
_____

CREATIVITY
Expression Yourself

"You can't use up creativity. The more you use, the more you have."

Maya Angelou

Creativity isn't a limited resource—it's a renewable spark. The more you engage it, the more it expands. Every time you express, explore, or invent, you open new doors inside yourself.

What's one creative idea you've been holding back—and what might happen if you let it out?

_____

_____

_____

_____

_____

_____

_____

_____

_____

_____

71. Your body is your home—treat it with love.

Your body isn't a trend to be judged or fixed. It carries you, protects you, and reflects your lived experience. Nourish it, rest it, celebrate it. You live here.

What's one kind thing you can do for your body today?

_____

_____

_____

_____

_____

_____

_____

_____

_____

_____

_____

_____

_____

_____

_____

72. Movement is medicine.

You don't have to be an athlete to move your body with care. Whether dancing, walking, stretching, or playing—movement helps you process emotions, release stress, and return to yourself.

What kind of movement feels joyful or freeing for you—and how can you make space for it?

_____

_____

_____

_____

_____

_____

_____

_____

_____

_____

_____

_____

_____

73. Sleep is sacred.

Your brain and body need deep rest to function, heal, and grow. Prioritizing sleep is an act of self-respect. Protect it like the treasure it is.

How could you protect your sleep as if your well-being depends on it—because it does?

_____

_____

_____

_____

_____

_____

_____

_____

_____

_____

_____

_____

_____

_____

_____

74. Nourishment is more than food—it's fuel for your future.

Food isn't about guilt or rules—it's about honoring your body's needs. Eat to feel strong, grounded, and energized. Your body deserves kindness and balance.

What would it look like to eat in a way that honors your body, not punishes it?

_____

_____

_____

_____

_____

_____

_____

_____

_____

_____

_____

_____

_____

_____

75. Hydration affects everything.

Water keeps your mind clear, your skin glowing, and your body in harmony. It's a small act of care with a big impact. Drink up.

How can you make drinking water a consistent act of self-care?

_____

_____

_____

_____

_____

_____

_____

_____

_____

_____

_____

_____

_____

_____

76. Your body's signals are worth listening to.

Your fatigue, your pain, your hunger—they're not annoyances; they're messages. When you tune in, you learn how to support yourself better.

What signal has your body been sending lately—and are you paying attention?

_____

_____

_____

_____

_____

_____

_____

_____

_____

_____

_____

_____

_____

_____

_____

77. You are more than your appearance.

Your beauty isn't defined by mirrors or media. It's in how you treat others, how you carry yourself, and how you show up in the world. Don't let a reflection determine your worth.

What qualities define your worth beyond how you look?

_____

_____

_____

_____

_____

_____

_____

_____

_____

_____

_____

_____

_____

78. Health is holistic.

Mental, emotional, spiritual, and physical wellness are all connected. Caring for one part of yourself helps all the others. You're a whole being.

Which area of your wellness—mental, emotional, physical, or spiritual—needs more care right now?

_____

_____

_____

_____

_____

_____

_____

_____

_____

_____

_____

_____

_____

_____

_____

79. Rest is productive.

Doing nothing isn't laziness—it's healing. Rest restores creativity, focus, and joy. Take breaks not because you've earned them, but because you're human.

How can you reframe rest as something necessary, not indulgent?

_____

_____

_____

_____

_____

_____

_____

_____

_____

_____

_____

_____

_____

_____

_____

_____

_____

80. Your body deserves your gratitude, not your judgment.

Thank it for what it's carried you through. Your body hears your thoughts. Speak to it with love, and it will respond with strength.

What has your body carried you through that deserves your thanks today?

_____

_____

_____

_____

_____

_____

_____

_____

_____

_____

_____

_____

_____

_____

CHALLENGES
Mistakes & Growth

"Out of difficulties grow miracles."

– Jean de La Bruyère

Hard times often feel like the end—but they can be the beginning of something unexpected and powerful. Growth doesn't always look like success at first.

It reminds you that challenges can be the soil for transformation—and hope can grow even in the darkest places.

What difficulty have you faced that led to something beautiful, surprising, or healing?

_____

_____

_____

_____

_____

_____

_____

_____

81. Creativity is your birthright.

You were born to imagine, build, express, and explore. Creativity isn't reserved for artists—it's in how you solve problems, tell stories, and dream. Trust your ideas—they come from somewhere true.

What creative idea or impulse have you been ignoring—and what's one way to explore it?

_____

_____

_____

_____

_____

_____

_____

_____

_____

_____

_____

_____

_____

_____

_____

82. There's no wrong way to express yourself.

Whether it's through poetry, fashion, music, or silence—your way of expressing yourself is valid. Don't let fear of judgment dim your light. Be weird, be wild, be you.

What's one thing you'd express if fear of judgment disappeared?

_____

_____

_____

_____

_____

_____

_____

_____

_____

_____

_____

_____

_____

_____

_____

83. Your voice matters—even when it shakes.

Speaking your truth is powerful, especially when it's hard. Your vulnerability is not weakness—it's strength. Every time you use your voice; you make space for others to do the same.

What truth do you need to speak—even if your voice trembles?

_____

_____

_____

_____

_____

_____

_____

_____

_____

_____

_____

_____

_____

84. Art heals.

Creating something with your hands, heart, or imagination helps you process emotions that words alone can't reach. Let art be your outlet and your medicine.

What creative outlet helps you process emotions when words fall short?

_____

_____

_____

_____

_____

_____

_____

_____

_____

_____

_____

_____

_____

_____

85. You don't have to monetize every passion.

It's okay to do things simply because they bring you joy. Not everything needs to become a side hustle. Your joy is enough reason.

What's something you love doing simply for the joy of it?

_____

_____

_____

_____

_____

_____

_____

_____

_____

_____

_____

_____

_____

_____

86. Music moves emotions.

Music can lift you, calm you, or help you cry when words fail. Let playlists become your therapy sessions, your time capsules, your personal anthems.

What song always shifts your emotional state—and when did you last let music move you?

_____

_____

_____

_____

_____

_____

_____

_____

_____

_____

_____

_____

_____

_____

_____

_____

_____

87. Journaling is self-care.

Writing down your thoughts makes room inside your head. It helps you process, reflect, and grow. A journal is a mirror for your mind and a friend that always listens.

What thoughts are swirling in your mind that need a place to land on paper?

_____

_____

_____

_____

_____

_____

_____

_____

_____

_____

_____

_____

_____

_____

_____

88. You are allowed to evolve creatively.

Your style, your voice, your ideas—they're meant to change. Don't box yourself in with who you were last year. Growth is part of the artistic journey.

How has your creativity changed—and how can you honor that evolution?

_____

_____

_____

_____

_____

_____

_____

_____

_____

_____

_____

_____

_____

_____

_____

_____

89. Sharing your work is an act of courage.

It's brave to say, 'I made this.' Every time you share something you created; you're choosing vulnerability over fear. That's powerful.

What's one thing you've created that you're proud of—and who might you share it with?

_____

_____

_____

_____

_____

_____

_____

_____

_____

_____

_____

_____

_____

_____

90. You are art in motion.

Your existence is a masterpiece in progress. From your quirks to your courage, you're shaping something no one else in the world could ever replicate.

In what ways are you a living expression of your own unique beauty?

_____

_____

_____

_____

_____

_____

_____

_____

_____

_____

_____

_____

_____

_____

SPIRITUALITY
Wonder & Mystery

"There are more things in Heaven and Earth... than are dreamt of in your philosophy."

— Shakespeare

This quote invites you to embrace mystery, wonder, and humility. No matter how much you think you understand, the universe is always bigger, deeper, and more magical than you can imagine. It's a reminder to stay curious, open, and aware that not everything can be explained—but it can still be experienced.

When was the last time something surprised you, amazed you, or made you believe in something more?

_____

_____

_____

_____

_____

_____

_____

91. Mistakes are part of mastery.

No one gets it right the first time. Mistakes don't mean you're failing—they mean you're learning. Every great artist, athlete, or thinker started out unsure. Keep going.

What mistake helped you improve or understand something better?

_____

_____

_____

_____

_____

_____

_____

_____

_____

_____

_____

_____

_____

_____

_____

92. Failure isn't final—it's feedback.

When something doesn't work out, it's not the end—it's information. What worked? What didn't? What will you do differently next time? That's how you grow.

What's a "failure" you can now view as a valuable lesson?

_____

_____

_____

_____

_____

_____

_____

_____

_____

_____

_____

_____

_____

_____

_____

93. Resilience is a skill you build over time.

You don't have to be unbreakable to be strong. Every time you bounce back, even if slowly, you build emotional muscle. Resilience is built through practice, not perfection.

What's a time you bounced back—and what did it reveal about your strength?

_____
_____
_____
_____
_____
_____
_____
_____
_____
_____
_____
_____
_____
_____

94. Your past does not define your future.

What happened before may have shaped you, but it doesn't get to dictate who you become. You are allowed to change, to grow, to heal—and to write a new story.

What part of your past are you ready to stop letting define your next steps?

_____

_____

_____

_____

_____

_____

_____

_____

_____

_____

_____

_____

_____

_____

95. You are not your worst moment.

One decision, one outburst, one mistake doesn't make you unworthy. You are the sum of your actions, yes—but also your intentions, your repair, and your capacity to evolve.

What's one part of your story that deserves forgiveness or re-framing?

_____

_____

_____

_____

_____

_____

_____

_____

_____

_____

_____

_____

_____

_____

_____

96. Growth comes from being uncomfortable.

Comfort zones are cozy but limiting. True growth happens when you stretch—when you try, risk, stumble, and keep going anyway. Lean into discomfort—it's where transformation lives.

What discomfort are you currently navigating—and what growth might be waiting on the other side?

_____

_____

_____

_____

_____

_____

_____

_____

_____

_____

_____

_____

_____

_____

97. Courage isn't the absence of fear—it's action in spite of it.

You don't have to wait to be fearless to be brave. Courage is moving forward even with a racing heart. You're already braver than you think.

What's something brave you could do—even if fear is still present?

_____

_____

_____

_____

_____

_____

_____

_____

_____

_____

_____

_____

_____

98. Self-compassion fuels progress.

Being hard on yourself doesn't make you stronger—it makes you scared. Talk to yourself the way you would talk to a friend. Kindness creates the safety to grow.

What would it sound like to talk to yourself with gentleness instead of criticism?

_____
_____
_____
_____
_____
_____
_____
_____
_____
_____
_____
_____
_____
_____
_____
_____

99. You are a work in progress—and that's beautiful.

You don't need to be finished to be valuable. You're allowed to be messy and magnificent at the same time. Honor who you are becoming.

What part of your journey are you learning to embrace—flaws and all?

_____

_____

_____

_____

_____

_____

_____

_____

_____

_____

_____

_____

_____

_____

_____

100. There's always more to learn, love, and become.

Life isn't about reaching a destination—it's about staying curious, open, and alive along the way. Keep growing, keep reaching, keep becoming—you're just getting started.

What's one way you can stay open to becoming more of who you truly are?

_____
_____
_____
_____
_____
_____
_____
_____
_____
_____
_____
_____
_____
_____

QUOTES FROM ACROSS THE AGES

"Happiness depends upon ourselves."

Aristotle

"The best way to predict the future is to create it."

Abraham Lincoln

"Act as if what you do makes a difference. It does."

William James

"It always seems impossible until it's done."

Nelson Mandela

"Success is not final; failure is not fatal: it is the courage to continue that counts."

Winston Churchill

"Keep your face always toward the sunshine—and shadows will fall behind you."

Walt Whitman

"You are never too old to set another goal or to dream a new dream."

C.S. Lewis

"Believe you can and you're halfway there."

Theodore Roosevelt

"Try to be a rainbow in someone's cloud."

Maya Angelou

"Do what you can, with what you have, where you are."

Theodore Roosevelt

"Be yourself; everyone else is already taken."

Oscar Wilde

"Be the change that you wish to see in the world."

Mahatma Gandhi

"In the middle of every difficulty lies opportunity."

Albert Einstein

"If you want to lift yourself up, lift up someone else."
Booker T. Washington

"Every strike brings me closer to the next home run."
Babe Ruth

"You miss 100% of the shots you don't take."

Wayne Gretzky

"Whether you think you can or you think you can't, you're right."

Henry Ford

"Opportunities don't happen. You create them."

Chris Grosser

"Don't watch the clock; do what it does. Keep going."

Sam Levenson

"It's not whether you get knocked down. It's whether you get up."

Vince Lombardi

"What you get by achieving your goals is not as important as what you become by achieving your goals."

Zig Ziglar

"Everything you've ever wanted is on the other side of fear."

George Addair

"Dream big and dare to fail."

Norman Vaughan

"Go confidently in the direction of your dreams. Live the life you have imagined."

Henry David Thoreau

"Life is 10% what happens to us and 90% how we react to it."

Charles R. Swindoll

"The mind is everything. What you think you become."
Buddha

"You must do the thing you think you cannot do."

Eleanor Roosevelt

"Make each day your masterpiece."

John Wooden

"Wherever you go, go with all your heart."

Confucius

"Try not to become a person of success but rather try to become a person of value."

Albert Einstein

"Do not go where the path may lead, go instead where there is no path and leave a trail."

Ralph Waldo Emerson

"We can do anything we want to if we stick to it long enough."

Helen Keller

"The only limit to our realization of tomorrow is our doubts of today."

Franklin D. Roosevelt

"Life isn't about finding yourself. Life is about creating yourself."

George Bernard Shaw

"What lies behind us and what lies before us are tiny matters compared to what lies within us."

Ralph Waldo Emerson

"If you're going through hell, keep going."

Winston Churchill

"Act the way you'd like to be and soon you'll be the way you act."

Leonard Cohen

"The harder the conflict, the greater the triumph."

George Washington

"He who has a why to live can bear almost any how."

Friedrich Nietzsche

"When you arise in the morning, think of what a precious privilege it is to be alive."

Marcus Aurelius

"Knowing yourself is the beginning of all wisdom."

Aristotle

"We are made wise not by the recollection of our past, but by the responsibility for our future."

George Bernard Shaw

"Don't count the days, make the days count."

Muhammad Ali

"Peace begins with a smile."

Mother Teresa

"Do not dwell in the past, do not dream of the future, concentrate the mind on the present moment."

Buddha

"The secret of getting ahead is getting started."

Mark Twain

"Happiness is not something ready-made. It comes from your own actions."

Dalai Lama

"We cannot solve problems with the same thinking we used when we created them."

Albert Einstein

"Only in the darkness can you see the stars."

Martin Luther King Jr.

"Do not let what you cannot do interfere with what you can do."

John Wooden

"All our dreams can come true, if we have the courage to pursue them."

Walt Disney

"Don't be pushed around by the fears in your mind. Be led by the dreams in your heart."

Roy T. Bennett

"Don't let yesterday take up too much of today."

Will Rogers

"It does not matter how slowly you go as long as you do not stop."

Confucius

"A journey of a thousand miles begins with a single step."

Lao Tzu

"You have power over your mind—not outside events. Realize this, and you will find strength."

Marcus Aurelius

"When we strive to become better than we are, everything around us becomes better too."

Paulo Coelho

"Success is getting what you want. Happiness is wanting what you get."

Dale Carnegie

"Live as if you were to die tomorrow. Learn as if you were to live forever."

Mahatma Gandhi

"Every day may not be good… but there is something good in every day."

Alice Morse Earle

"The best preparation for tomorrow is doing your best today."

H. Jackson Brown Jr.

"Success is how high you bounce when you hit bottom."

George S. Patton

"Keep looking up… that's the secret of life."

Charlie Brown (Charles M. Schulz)

"The greatest glory in living lies not in never falling, but in rising every time we fall."

Nelson Mandela

"You may not be perfect, but you are perfectly you."

Christopher Graham